LIGHTNING BOLT BOOKS™

V

Ninja Competitions

Laura Hamilton Waxman

Lerner Publications • Minneapolis

Lerner Publications Company
An imprint of Lerner Publishing Group, Inc.
241 First Avenue North
Minneapolis, MN 55401 USA

For reading levels and more information, look up this title at www.lernerbooks.com.

Library of Congress Cataloging-in-Publication Data

Names: Waxman, Laura Hamilton, author.
Title: Ninja competitions / Laura Hamilton Waxman.
Description: Minneapolis : Lerner Publishing Group, 2020. | Series: Lightning bolt books: Ninja mania | Includes bibliographical references and index. | Audience: Grades 2-3 | Audience: Ages 6-9 | Summary: "At ninja competitions, athletes jump, climb, and flip their way through a twisted obstacle course. Explore the history behind the wild sport of ninja and its connection to ninja of the past"— Provided by publisher.
Identifiers: LCCN 2019026108 (print) | LCCN 2019026109 (ebook) | ISBN 9781541577053 (library binding) | ISBN 9781541589162 (paperback) | ISBN 9781541583252 (pdf)
Subjects: LCSH: Ninjutsu—Juvenile literature. | Martial arts—Japan—Juvenile literature. | Ninja—Juvenile literature.
Classification: LCC GV1114.73 .W39 2020 (print) | LCC GV1114.73 (ebook) | DDC 796.815/2—dc23

LC record available at https://lccn.loc.gov/2019026108
LC ebook record available at https://lccn.loc.gov/2019026109

Manufactured in the United States of America
1-46727-47718-8/26/2019

Table of Contents

Strength and Smarts

The crowd at the ninja competition roars with excitement. They are watching someone leap, climb, and dash through an obstacle course.

Ninja athletes practice tackling many types of obstacles.

People in ninja competitions must be strong, quick, and smart. They need to move their bodies skillfully to succeed. So did ninja of the past.

Real ninja lived hundreds of years ago in Japan. They were strong and stealthy spies. Ninja were most common in the fifteenth to seventeenth centuries. This was a time of war in Japan.

Powerful Japanese families hired ninja to spy on their enemies.

The show *American Ninja Warrior* is based on *Sasuke.*

Ninja competitions grew out of a love for all things ninja. The sport began in Japan in the 1990s on the *Sasuke* TV show. Similar competitions soon spread to the United States and other countries.

Myth vs. Reality

Many people think that real ninja were warriors who fought with sharp swords. But they most often worked as spies and scouts. They tried not to get into fights.

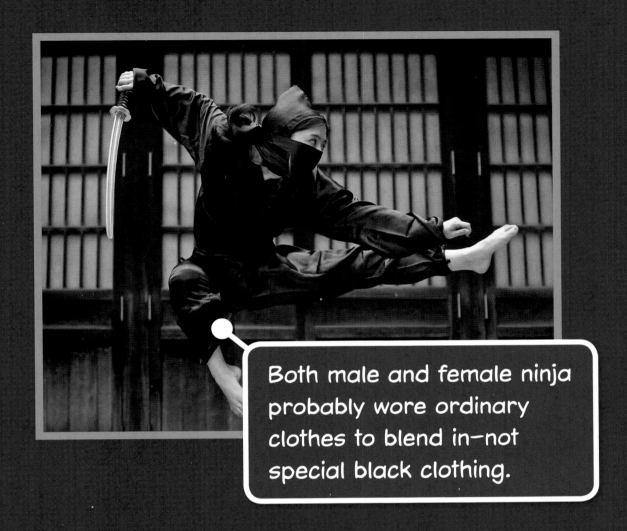

Both male and female ninja probably wore ordinary clothes to blend in—not special black clothing.

Like ninja competitors, real ninja had tough minds and strong bodies. Historically, ninja were mostly men. Some stories also mention women ninja called *kunoichi*.

In movies and on TV, ninja always work at night. But ninja often spied during the day. They had to watch and listen without being seen.

Ninja of the past probably practiced climbing many different surfaces.

Ninja carefully snuck into enemy territory. They crawled through grass and swam across ponds and rivers. They climbed trees and slipped inside castles.

Ninja Skills

Ninja of the past had to train their bodies and minds so they could be good spies. Modern ninja competitors must also learn many skills to compete.

Ninja of the past did a lot of climbing. They sometimes used iron claws or hooked ropes to pull their bodies up castle walls. Ninja competitors must be strong climbers too. But they use only their hands!

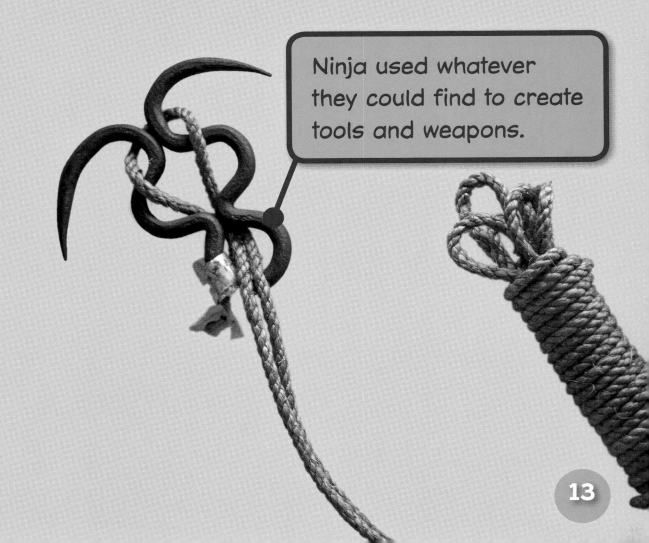

Ninja used whatever they could find to create tools and weapons.

Historical ninja knew how to walk and crawl without making a sound. Ninja competitors also control their bodies carefully. They must move through an obstacle course without falling or slowing down.

Modern ninja stengthen their bodies to get past obstacles.

Just like modern competitors, historical ninja amazed people with their many skills. Ninja were so stealthy and strong that people believed they had superpowers. Some even said that ninja could fly.

Sometimes modern ninja seem like they can fly too!

Ninja Competitions in Action

Ninja had to be fearless to carry out their spying missions. Modern ninja competitors need to be just as daring to succeed.

Ninja athletes train their minds and bodies, just as ninja from the past did.

Modern ninja competitors don't crawl through grass, climb castles, or run across enemy lines. They climb ropes and ladders, jump over water, and race to the finish line.

Kids get in on the action too. Young competitors train for and compete in ninja races all over the country. A junior ninja competition is even on TV.

Some US soldiers train like ninja too.

Ninja competitors of any age are tough and determined. Like real-life ninja, they inspire people with their strength, skill, and bravery.

Real-Life Ninja

Some say Mochizuki Chiyome was the first female ninja. She lived in Japan in the sixteenth century. Stories say she married a warrior who belonged to a powerful family. This family fought wars with other powerful families to control parts of Japan.

When Chiyome's husband died in battle, his family asked if she'd organize a band of *kunoichi* to help them. Chiyome said yes. She searched for women who could be spies. Then she either found male ninja to train them or trained them herself. This team of women kept Chiyome's family safe.

Ninja Fun Facts

- In Japan, ninja were called *shinobi*.

- After the wars in Japan ended, ninja mostly disappeared. But their stories still amazed the Japanese people. Those stories reached the United States in the twentieth century.

- People all over the world watched the Japanese ninja competitions on *Sasuke*. The show *American Ninja Warrior* is based on *Sasuke*.

Glossary

competitor: someone who takes part in a competition

mission: a job given to a spy, such as spying on an enemy's army

obstacle course: a race filled with challenges a competitor must overcome

scout: someone who secretly explores enemy land to find out where important things and places are

stealthy: hidden or secretive

territory: land controlled by a leader, landowner, or country

Further Reading

Are Ninjas Real?
https://www.wonderopolis.org/wonder/are-ninjas
-real

Davies, Beth. *Ninja in Action!* New York: DK, 2018.

Doudna, Kelly. *Ninjas! Skilled and Stealthy Secret Agents*. Minneapolis: Abdo, 2018.

Moon, Walt K. *Let's Explore Japan.* Minneapolis: Lerner Publications, 2017.

National Geographic Kids: Japan
https://kids.nationalgeographic.com/explore
/countries/japan/#japan-gardens.jpg

Terp, Gail. *Ninja.* Mankato, MN: Black Rabbit Books, 2020.

Index

Photo Acknowledgments

Image credits: NicolasMcComber/Getty Images, p. 2; Emma McIntyre/Getty Images, pp. 4, 7; U.S. Air Force/Staff Sgt. Stephenie Wade), p. 5; Library of Congress, p. 6; Katsushika Hokusai, *Tenji Tenno (The Emperor Tenji)*, 1830-1841. The Art Institute of Chicago, p. 8; 1001nights/ Getty Images, p. 9; emyerson/Getty Images, p. 10; BLOOM image/Getty Images, p. 11; U.S. Air Force/Samuel King Jr, p. 12; Paak Tripaakwasin/Shutterstock.com, p. 13; Vyacheslav Prokofyev/TASS/Getty Images, p. 14; Hyoung Chang/The Denver Post/Getty Images, p. 15; Rodin Eckenroth/Getty Images, p. 16; Tommaso Boddi/WireImage/Getty Images, p. 17; U.S. Air Force/Naoto Anazawa, p. 18; U.S. Marine Corps/Lance Cpl. Connor Hancock, p. 19; 4x6/ Getty Images, p. 22.

Cover: Seth McConnell/The Denver Post/Getty Images.

Main body text set in Billy Infant regular. Typeface provided by SparkType.